MARMALADE

ALSO BY WILLIAM BENTON

POETRY

The Bell Poems
Birds
Eye La View
L'aprè-midi d'un faune
Normal Meanings
Marmalade
A Quatrain on Sleeping Beauty's Tomb
    (TRANSLATIONS FROM BORIS PASTERNAK)
Backlit
Light on Water, New and Selected Poems

PROSE

Exchanging Hats: Elizabeth Bishop Paintings
Deaf Elephants (CHILDREN'S BOOK)
Madly (NOVEL)
The Mary Julia Paintings of Joan Brown
Reliquaries: The Sculpture of Ted Waltz

EDITOR

Gods of Tin: The Flying Years by James Salter

MARMALADE

Drifts, Gists, Versions, Drafts, and Takes

poems by
William Benton

drawings by
James McGarrell

Station Hill Press
BARRYTOWN, NY

Text © 1976, 1978, 1997, 2025 William Benton
Drawings © 1997 James McGarrell

All rights reserved. Except for short passages for purposes of review, no part of this book may be reproduced in any form or by any means, electronic or mechanical, including photocopying, recording, or by any information storage and retrieval system, without permission in writing from the publisher.

Published by Station Hill Press, the publishing project of the Institute for Publishing Arts, Inc., 120 Station Hill Road, Barrytown, NY 12507, New York, a not-for-profit, Federally tax-exempt organization [501(c)(3)].

Online catalogue: www.stationhill.org
E-mail: publishers@stationhill.org

This is an expanded edition of the book first published by George Adams Gallery Press (New York: 1997) and designed by Karen A. Ocker.

ACKNOWLEDGEMENTS

L'après-midi d'un faune was first published in a limited edition with drawings by David Authier and introduction by Guy Davenport (Pyramid Editions, Santa Fe). *Tristesse d'été, Petit air, Angoisse, Une négresse, Le crieur d'imprimés, Mes bouquins,* and *Quelle soir* were first published in the book *Normal Meanings* (Deer Crossing Press, Paducah). A limited edition portfolio of *Marmalade,* with original intaglio prints by James McGarrell, was first published by Elephants Foot Press, Peoria.

Library of Congress Catalog Card Number available on request.
ISBN: 978-1-58177-235-7

Land Acknowledgment

In the spirit of truth and equity, it is with gratitude and humility that we acknowledge that the Institute for Publishing Arts, Inc. and Station Hill Press reside on the sacred homelands of the Munsee and Muhheaconneok people, who are the original stewards of this land. Today, due to forced removal, the community resides in Northeast Wisconsin and is known as the Stockbridge-Munsee Community.

Contents

Introduction	ix
Quelle soie	3
Sainte	4
Angoisse	5
Petit air I	6
Le crieur d'imprimés	8
Toute l'âme résumée	9
Une négresse	10
Mes bouquins	11
L'après-midi d'un faune	13
Hèrodiade	20
Placet futile	26
Le tombeau d'Edgar Poe	27
M'introduire...	28
Autres poemes et sonnets	29
Petit air II	32
Tristesse d'été	33
Prose	35
Afterword	39
About the Author and Artist	41

For Joanne Kyger
(1934-2017)

Introduction*

A poem that, transposed by Debussy into musical phrases which follow Mallarmé syllable by syllable, Nijinsky could dance to for six-hundred-and-twenty-two seconds, crouched like a cheetah whose stalking body moved with the slowness of lava while the long muscles of his animal legs and back flexed in a liquid rhythm quicker than the dreaming flow of his dance, his Mongol eyes half closed in revery, a poem that Matisse accepted as a theme to study for half a century, that Valéry said was the most skillful in all French literature, that rewrites Theokritos psychologically as Cezanne repainted Poussin "from nature," that awakened in a cityscape of factories and shops a theme to entrance Picasso all of his old age, that comes as close as any work of art is ever likely to expressing the all but inexpressible interpenetration of world and mind, is worth translating if only to prove once again that it can't be done.

Huxley's translation turns Mallarme's sunstruck gold into correct English silver; Fry's transposes the color into an assiduously finished steel engraving. William Benton, full of the mischief of being exactly half serious, turns it into a primitive painting, like Horace Pippin copying Emmanuel Leutze's "Washington Crossing the Delaware."

---

* This is the inroduction to the 1976 edition of L'après-midi d'un faune.

Asked how you understand a poem, you paraphrase it ("thought is like a witness summoned into court, its sweetness was in its silence") to show what you think it says. If the poem is in another language, you translate ("the wild fury sing, Goddess, of Peleus's son Achilles ..."). William Benton does both.

Nouns are names to children and Aesop, so the faun becomes Le Faune. And the isolate and lordly satyr, philosopher and artist, becomes an adolescent gorgeously confusing biology and will. In Mallarmé this is an irony that parallels our best understanding of spontaneity and fate. In Benton it is a charming puzzle. Mallarmé seems to say that once the world fears our benevolence with predictable stupidity and depressing habit, we begin to doubt benevolence and trust our dreams. We take up our flute, our book, our old sweater with the elbows gone.

They don't, as far as we know, exist, these fauns. Like the perpetuable girls in the poem they come from the notes of a whistle, from the painter's brush, the sculptor's chisel. Never mind that Pausanias visited the grave of one in Syria. The Greek mind (a subject Mallarmé taught to insufferable French schoolboys, whose scribbled themes he read in despair) was capable of seeing their goat step among leaves, ramshorns curled, sharp of glance, Cnossan-eyed. Their musk preceded them, armpit and honeysuckle, quince flower descant upon a rackle of billy pizzle. Tuscan brown and the visages of Italic gods, their pentathletic torsos flowed with bestial grace into dappled haunches – the effect Bakst created for Nijinsky.

Stag tales frisking up from their holy bone wagged above the flat of their narrow butts.

They are recorded on thousands of jugs: munching an apple, buzzing their lips like a hornet, twiddling the radical of a stegacephallic *posthon*.

The Greeks would have supposed their knowledge of the gods to be intuitive, fretful, dark. Of Zeus they would have known the suddenness of lightning and the thunder's hackling of its neck, hateful winds, rain and snow. Artemis they would have known as Mother of Bears. Hera they did not know. Their Lord of the Dance was not Appollon but Pan, whom they probably called Humper. Asklepios was Snake, Demeter the apple, pear, and plum, Persephatta the poppy and the wren.

Their language was inhuman. They could chatter with squirrels, using squirrel *parole* among themselves to bound their peripatesis. For time they used the vocabulary of the grey wolf, for elegy and boast the nicker and whinny of the horse, for familiar discourse a patois of birdsong, fox bark, goat bleat, and the sniffle and mump of their cousins the deer.

Hesiod first mentions them, *the race of satyrs about which nothing can be done*. In Sicily they were called Tityrs. Silenos the friend of Dionysos was one of them, prophet and drunkard. There is Asia in this detail, a transference onto the leaf-god Dushara through whom the dead could speak of some shaman whose trance came from wine.

The true fauns were shy woods creatures whose only boldness was in mounting hamadryads, maelids, sheep and their snub-nosed shepherd, goats and their dark-eyed goatherd, country girls out berrying, pious wives at the spring, anything with penetrable *pterygomata* into which their urgent *saunia* might squeeze. Neither voluptuaries nor lovers, they never thought to mention in their gossip of weather and time with the wolves that the day had seen them chase and hump a nimble wife and her cow, a brace of oreads whom they found in each other's arms, a pasture of horses, and an hysterical swan.

And if one dreamed, and was too feral to sort dream from flesh, and took up a flute and began to see how dream and reality are flower and leaf on the one stem, and a French poet in a plaid shawl who loved old gardens and mirrors and Greek poetry wrote what he thought the faun thought, and an American poet has a bright impulse to speak for Mallarmé speaking for the faun? Turn the page and read on.

— GUY DAVENPORT

MARMALADE

QUELLE SOIE

What silk
that time.

Mirror
Chimera,

your hair
twists,

intends.
Loopholes

along our street
are raised

like flags.
Glories.

Love,
breathe out

in your cry
and in.

SAINTE

At the window
a saint stops by,
staining the glass.

ANGOISSE

She sweeps her hair
which is black,

      a squall

on the tropical sheet.

      *

"Tonight let's just go to sleep."

      *

Dawn... The ripe moments abandon themselves
and escape to the next, pale and exhausted.

      *

The breast is stone and haunted, heartless

as a tooth.

PETIT AIR

    I

Solitude, the medium
time occurs in,
then swans and the dark.

It passes from the mirror
out to the peering look of abdication:
then sky.

Stray plumes.
The sun's affectation
is the horizon — as yours is,

like the next gull if it dives,
an idea of her clothes off
happy and naked, white into white wave.

LE CRIEUR D'IMPRIMÉS

1.

Even in March the day's prophesies elude you.
The parks start to fill in pairs for the blank.
That newsboy goes by. Perhaps
only his height is half-empty, displacing an invisible
life, whatever the headlines.

2.

They meet in light green sunglasses. He stands
stranded where behind him the trees stop, an old man:
her fingers lift like a small sail.
She is young and probably calls it 'the sniffles',
but he doesn't know. Everything blurs but its joy.

TOUTE L'ÂME RÉSUMÉE

Truly
q-t adventures,
day-dreams
and smoky places.

A test is
best. Its clear kiss
quivers and
dies

after
a song. Lips move
exactly right, beginning to see the
light.

Lit: it copies you in-
to shadows.

UNE NÉGRESSE

        She is not herself
today and wants to fuck. The little
boy says, "O.K.", because of her clothes which
have underneath them the big tits and so fat.

                Then she goes
subsequently and barooms down all ober, it is
the green earth, and bounces, the dust leaps
then, and she is looping backwards the loop,
as it rises, a shiny tangle, roaming the sky,
and she nestles his hand.

              The crazy elephant.

Dim eyes and her grin. He hops onto the, oh,
he is happening like a gazelle. And they are
          over the ocean
      pale and rosy

as a shell on its floor.

MES BOUQUINS

The books closed with Paphos.
Waves in a single stroke
arrive and build ruins.

Hyacinth days.

      It was over
the ground, about honor, any landscape
can be unreal and is entitled to be.

The apples and turtles.

Our feet wade, cold as snow.
I am distracted and brood.
The other one has tanned breasts, like an Amazon.

L'APRÈS-MIDI D'UN FAUNE

    Three carnations
one black and two red ones are arranged
       deftly, drowsy vaginas
aroused by the stems of flowers, awaken the nymphs. . . .

Le Faune arrives
on the scene. He pauses
in a small meadow
and rubs his eyes. But what happened was
a great commotion was ensuing, and
an animal whiteness mingled
now with something seen for an instant
it fled through the branches.
Le Faune felt
this was awful. For he
thought the girls very beautiful and wanted
to fuck them. But now they
were gone. So, at length, he closed his eyes,
to sleep in the soft grass of the meadow. And
one by one, the beautiful girls
took shape in the dark of his eyes.
For a time
he loved the dream. Yet it caused him
to look again forlornly at the empty meadow.
He had, he knew, but one hope which was to chase
into the forest after the beautiful girls. But
then he wondered, *which forest?* Now,
there were two forests,
and one was real and one was
the other one. Le Faune was so confused
that he didn't go into either of the forests. He went
to a little garden
bordering on the meadow. And there
he sat down and offered
to himself, as a small triumph,
the ideal lack
of roses.

Poor Le Faune set about ordering his thoughts.
He wanted to follow the beautiful girls.
He thought of the two forests, each with silver
and black leaves, surrounding the garden.
Where, where, where was the nature of his hard thoughts.
Where did they go? He scratched his head.
Oh no, cried Le Faune out loud. Not in *there*, he
protested.

But they were.

Well then if that is so pondered Le Faune,
                    and he forgot
about the two forests, shimmering in the sunlight
    assuming wrongly that the journey was to be
          unfraught with complexities, and that soon
safe inside his own head he would find only
                the beautiful girls. How could
  he have known differently? There was no one
to tell Le Faune. But then
     he chanced upon a Weeping Spring in the woods.
          Actually
it was somewhere in between the real woods and the
other, but when Le Faune came upon it it wept
    from blue eyes
  which, he realized, were his own,
                     and he wept too. Sadly
he saw the journey had begun and he was lost.
    Oh, well. He would speak to the Weeping
      Spring with the twin-pipes
of his flute. He was surprised, hearing
the notes turn into a lovely song, uncomplaining
     because here
  the music floated on the water
  and he had become himself the Wind having travelled
a little bit. Thus encouraged, he went on in his song
   about the Water and the Wind and the Trees
     saying that those things came to exist because
            this was that song
in which they were *inspired* sort of like *it* was, which,
 it said,

     regained the sky.

Sitting under the sky, Le Faune saw what had happened.
He was back in the little garden, at the edge of the
meadow.

    Capitulating, he mused upon his adventures:
        I was pretending to be
the sun, up over the flowering world
        a moment ago.
               Just then the light
    brightened all about him
and he saw that the white flowers, growing
 from the earth, had become precious to
    the sunlight. It was a quest
  not unlike his own, as the sun glanced off
    the white bodies Le Faune saw
      in the flowers. Sun woke them.
And they fluttered away, like Naiads.
        That was the *song* he had heard,
    when he spoke to the Weeping Spring!

Thus, the journey returned to Le Faune. He felt
    the song stalking him
  like a traitress, dressed in a raiment
      woven of leaves.

From his death,
Le Faune entered again
the glittering woods. All around
him the leaves parted, and there on a small hillock
were the beautiful girls. His mind
played quickly over the two sisters awakened
by the red flowers
and they met, entwined by embraces, as his mind rose
over them and up to the place where, it seemed,
the sun was. The powerful black carnation
of his mind grew like a star
on the sun's face. And Le Faune picked up
the twin-pipes. He wanted only to play a single note
from the intricate design of the song which the sun
knew. It was *la*. And it was the note in which the escape
of the beautiful girls took place
in the song. As he played it, he knew
also that it was the note in which no one could ever
know the secret of how the beautiful girls always had fled.
He played, it was
a long solo, proud of its noise, wrested
from the silvery-black husks of leaves
luminous in the evening sky.

So that is how, in the note, they escape.

From his lips.

HÉRODIADE

A blackbird flies

into the day, extinguishing stars.

It is a crime the sky had to be purple.

NO SPLASHING!

    signed,

The Purple Accomplice.

On the wing of a vanity
a bottle of Old Snows effaces the tacky giltwood.

The red window, wide open.

Her ideas
bunch into flowers. Their long stems and regret.

A lone vase. Lavender
ink.

I swan.

A voice trails flickerings of tiny gold stars, yellow folds of old thought, and cloth.

                        It comes thru holes,
an old veiled brilliance, toneless,

                    without acolyte
               yet. This scuffle

  here for power that speaks.

Daddy's out there praising the audacity of an earthly death.

She sings sometimes incoherently.

                      Blue Moon.
            Glimpsed in an orchard of pomegranates.

          He does not know of this, the king
          her father, too bad.

                The black pines
begin to silver at their tops and she walks around by herself,

      la, la, la, la.

PLACET FUTILE

I have zee heebie-jeebies.
Perhaps you shouldn't eat
that banana right now it's
gooing up your lipstick.

I was just thinking. Since
I am not him, where is that
little dog of yours, anyway?
You have very pretty hair.

No manure. It's like your laugh,
which is sacrilegious and
at the same time, innocent.

Here, let me tickle you
there. On the couch. Take
off your shoes, my darling.

LE TOMBEAU D'EDGAR POE

   Heaven and earth
    a bas-relief
to adorn Poe

  down here.

M'INTRODUIRE...

The red Vespa's
finished, rims &
wheels scattered

like a sunset. *The Thunder
of Ruby Goes to Heaven.*
I'm even happy.

It was very loud. I don't
deny its a hindrance,
but all in all I like
Glacier National Park's

high brassy meadows
where, if I go naked, it is
much as a hero
to bring myself into your attention.

AUTRES POEMES ET SONNETS

I

I loved it
when the whole night
was found out
and was openly

on fire. He's
dear: torch songs and smoke
from immortal
cigarettes,

who lives
inside
an ancient bedroom
unwarmed,

even if he comes
in from the corridor
with another
fallen blonde.

II

The line stops
without flowers.

I don't believe two mouths
ever knew the same kiss
they seemed to have in common.

The vase just sits there with
what it does not contain
in it.

PETIT AIR

    II

Up about
a way again.

Yanking a leg from the table
he stands up. Unrushed. Simpering
glamour

does not.
wish to be.

Where is the damn bird?

Where is that which nevermore could
in life be heard.

TRISTESSE D'ÉTÉ

Agile. On the white beach her hips.
The heat curls into air like incense,
where she sleeps, and dries her hair.

*

Out loud, he addresses herself and the sea:
will we be simpler to one another then?
the comic palms ancient and happier?

*

Little lights of sweat glisten
and go out in her hair. She wrestles
with a dream of lime popsicles.

*

He kisses misty streaks of mascara,
and draws in the sand a heart
which is blue and the color of stone.

PROSE
For Elaine

"High, purpley," murmured Stephane. He was looking
up a word in the dictionary. Humming and Sighing.
This happened to him frequently. He couldn't spell.
Irretrievable time it seemed piled up like ironing.

Stephane was writing a story. Outside a breeze
rushed through the twilight and lilacs. It played
softly over his desk. He watched the sky fade
and first stars rise above the tops of palm trees.

"Oh, look!" Stephane's sister — a slim, utopian
girl — stood with her back to the landscape. (Wild
forsythia and the white surrounding oleanders.) He
thought of the world, and then the world of her.

"Uh oh," Stephane remarked. It was a yellow
summery day in the life of the author. He went on,
"The mind writing about itself is the absence
of flowers — it notes — and presently troubled."

Thus Stephane slept in a bed of a hundred irises.
It was funny. I don't know really if it ever
existed. It was somewhere down south. A little
place to remain nameless. Except for a hint:

it's on an island. "The flowers are freer here,"
Stephane explained. "You avoid the cost of making
them up when you can look right at them in person."
Saying that, Stephane noticed how the flowers

all were commonly adorned with clear outlines.
He thought: the space between them is also
a space between them and the garden itself — the
distance of space — which waves hi at us.

Stephane's children spent their summers on
the island. They were like clear ideas to him.
The faces of a disk, spinning in sunlight.
They went for walks, cooked, spoke English.

That is with the exception of his sensible sister.
Tenderly, she declined, and would go no further than
to spare a smile. She had always been the bright
one. Stephane made things up to understand her.

He made up a stalk of asphodels. That greeny flower.
It was too tall though, taller than reason grew, anyhow
Stephane's. Still he left it as it was. It was late,
and a spirit of contention shivered in the air.

Meanwhile, the shore wept. Waves in monotonous
succession wrote white lines of prose.
Stephane's childhood dog, Sandy, barks at them
harmlessly, and at Stephane. You can just hear him.

Beside a glittering sea, Stephane is caught
between the sky and the map. A wave ebbs
away. His footsteps in the sand attest to his
complexity. "This island never existed," he says.

Appozee, his sister, drove back to the mainland
over the boring bridge between it and the island.
"For Garden Seed," she said, and thought: he was
born to be a goddamn book. That was Stephane.

Like their silly names, their love for each other.
It is an effort for Stephane to say this.
He stands watching the car, as it retreats
across light green fields, somewhere in France.

AFTERWORD

I first read Mallarmé in an excerpt from *Un Coup de Des*, published as a double page spread in a magazine. Lines with eccentric indentations ran across the center divide. The two pages became, themselves, a physical enactment of the poem's content: sea waves, the sails of a boat, the wings of a gull. It was mesmerizing. You held in your hands the actual matter of the poem.

However, as I began to read the established translations of Mallarmé (I knew very little French), the dazzle vanished. The calibrations of language that seemed implicit in the originals were lost in turgid, looney tunes of English. Ghosts glittered behind the texts.

I began these translations a few years later. The earliest dates from 1975, the last from 1979 or '80. I didn't then know Yevtushenko's famous comment: "Translation is like a woman. If it is beautiful, it is not faithful. If it is faithful, it is most certainly not beautiful." But Pounds's *Homage to Sextus Propertius* and *Cathay* were a part of my history.

In the poetry world of the early 1970s, it was almost a dictum that every poem ought to be a redefining of how a poem is made. Translation imposes by necessity a similar demand. Certain risks and notions, like the fairy tale lilt of the faun's story or the external narrative woven into "Prose," became singular attributes of the English versions. I had no overall process in mind. Inspector Clouseau's cameo in "Placet Futile," is as much an intuitive element as the improvisions of "Hérodiade." At the same time, "Tristesse d' Été, "Petit Air," "Mes Bouquin," and others are, in varying degrees, straightforward translations, changed like water in a glass by a single drop of foreign essence.

Which may be only one's life. *Marmalade* is a kind of autobiography. Each poem was as central to my occasion as I could make it. That alone offered the hope of producing a readable equivalent.

—WB

About the Author and Artist

WILLIAM BENTON received his early training in music and worked as a jazz piano player before becoming a writer. His poetry has appeared in *The New Yorker*, *The Paris Review*, and other magazines. He is the author of nine books of poetry, including *Birds*, *Marmalade*, and *Backlit*, as well as *Exchanging Hats*, a book on the paintings of Elizabeth Bishop, and *Madly*, a novel. His most recent book is *Light on Water*, New and Selected Poems, from Marsh Hawk Press. He lives in New York City.

JAMES MCGARRELL's paintings are in the permanent collections of many institutions including the Metropolitan Museum, the Museum of Modern Art, and the Whitney Museum of American Art in New York City; The Hirshhorn Museum in Washington, D.C, and the Art Museums of New Orleans, Saint Louis, Santa Barbara, San Francisco, and Hamburg Germany. In 1995 he received the Jimmy Ernst lifetime achievement award of the American Academy of Arts and Letters. He died in 2020.

www.ingramcontent.com/pod-product-compliance
Lightning Source LLC
Chambersburg PA
CBHW040258090526
44586CB00030B/79